for Roger Bailey
who has similar interest in hewing tools.
9/22/99
Sam Manning

New England Masts and The King's Broad Arrow

by S. F. Manning

Thomas Murphy, Publisher
Summer Street
Kennebunk, Maine 04043

Library of Congress Catalog Card Number: 79-88623

International Standard Book Number: 0-932006-08-6

Cover design and book layout by the Author.

Printed by New Hampshire Printers, Somersworth, N. H.

Published simultaneously as a Museum monograph by the National Maritime Museum, London, England.

Contents

Part I: England

The Wooden Economy 3
England and the Baltic Source 5
Mast Woods 9
Growing Need 13

Part II: New England

New England Pines 19
Settlement, and the Beginnings of New England Trade 23
The Broad Arrow Policy 29
Enabling Acts 33
Gains and Abuses 37
Mast Agents and Surveyors 45

Select Bibliography 52

Maps

Northern Europe 2
New England and Atlantic Canada 18
The White Pine Belt 20
Exports and Returns — 1650 — 27

Illustrations*

The King's Broad Arrow ii
Bedding the Fall 6
Felling 10
Limbing 14
Hovels 22
Twitching 24
Snub Rope and Bridle Chains 28
Baulking 31
Town Square 36
Mast Landing 38
Mast Depot 40
Ton Timber 42
Mast Ships 44
Stern Port 46
The Hold 48
Departure 51

* Commissioned by Maine Public Broadcasting Network for the film documentary, "Home to the Sea." Full size copies of these sixteen log handling scenes may be obtained quite inexpensively. They're large: 16″ by 20″ between borders. The series covers nearly thirty feet of wall space unmatted. Write: Maritime Heritage, Box 722, Camden, Maine 04843 for price.

Acknowledgments

The complicated patterns of trade and war which precipitated British sovereign claim to the pines of North America are not easily dealt with in the space of a few pages. Nor are the pictorial details of an important woods industry now vanished almost without trace. With both the story and the pictures a good deal of learned help was needed to establish the accuracy and the simplicity being strived for. I wish to thank these contributors for their kind cooperation:

Mr. Eton F. Churchill, Producer of Maine Public Broadcasting Network's film documentary, "Home to the Sea," whose personal interest and encouragement brought the 16 log-handling scenes into being;

Mr. Basil Greenhill, marine historian, Director of the National Maritime Museum at Greenwich, England, for the objective scrutiny and the guidance with detail which he gave to the masting scenes prior to their film appearance;

The *National Fisherman,* which allowed me to circulate a reprint of the original "Broad Arrow" story published in its pages, Sept. and Oct., 1977;

Capt. W. J. L. Parker (USCG Ret.), marine historian, former seaman in sailing timber droghers, for reading the NF manuscript and lending judgement to the pictorial content;

Prof. Clifford Chater of the Waltham Field Station, for pointing out the discrepancy between the botanical and the common names of mast trees as given in the classic sources;

Dr. J. P. Knight, Custodian of Manuscripts, National Maritime Museum, Greenwich, England, for his help in expanding the NF "Broad Arrow" story to the scope of this publication as well as for a British Maritime Museum monograph on the subject;

Dr. Charles F. Carroll, author of a source book important to this presentation, for his reading of the present manuscript and his helpful criticism of it;

and Susan H. Manning, my wife, able dorymate, research assistant and administrator of coffee throughout the whole effort.

The King's Broad Arrow

This was the ancient mark applied to British naval property. Three lines or cuts coming together as an arrow point with the apex upward. A tree which bore this mark in colonial New England was a white pine suitable for a mast in an English man-of-war. If you cut it down for any purpose other than delivery to the King's mast agent, you were liable for a fine of £100 per tree illegally cut.

About this story . . .

During the fall and winter of 1976 I was commissioned by the Maine Public Broadcasting Network to draw 16 scenes relating to the colonial mast trade which laid the foundations for lumbering and shipbuilding in Maine thereafter. The pictures were to be used in the opening minutes of an hour-long TV documentary titled "Home to the Sea." The film, a Bicentennial celebration of Maine's maritime heritage, was released during the summer of 1977.

It was a tantalizing assignment because MPBN's research effort in the Maine Archives had uncovered a certain amount of contemporary commentary relating to the once all-important mast trade, but no pictures of any kind that could be identified with it. There was very little description of mast-logging activity that an illustrator could work from. Film Producer Eton Churchill, himself a writer on Maine history, was able to send me to the places where mast logging had been done. Gorham, Maine was chosen for the tree-cutting and baulking scenes because a near-contemporary account of mast logging on pioneer farmland can be found in Elija Kellogg's *Good Old Times*. The mast route from Gorham led into the marshes at Stroudwater on Portland's Fore River. Thence, with the tide, to a mast house which once was situated just downriver from the crumbling abutment of old Route 1 bridge on Portland neck. Sketches were made and shown to old time Maine loggers, ox drovers, and shipwrights as well as seamen who had freighted big timber in the last days of commercial sail. Corrected drafts were sent to the National Maritime Museum at London, England, for the detailed overview which the

British historians could give us. When completed, the sixteen scenes represented the combined thinking of a good many knowledgeable people.

The scale of the mast logging operation, and its impact on England then, and North America later, was pieced together back in the 1920's by Robert G. Albion, a distinguished marine historian. This definitive work went between covers as *Forests and Sea Power: The Timber Problem of the Royal Navy, 1652-1862,* (1926). The book has a long chapter which explores the Broad Arrow Policy as it applied to North America. Another full chapter on the subject can be found in William Hutchinson Rowe's, *The Maritime History of Maine,* (1948). The forests of early England and the conditions which led to their demise; the forests of presettlement New England and the Yankee industries which they supported are both examined in colorful detail in Charles F. Carroll's *The Timber Economy of Puritan New England,* (1973). *Tall Trees, Tough Men,* a 1967 book by Robert E. Pike, highlights the basic facts of the Broad Arrow Policy and gives a penetrating look at how the big timbers were actually handled in the woods and on the rivers.

The Broad Arrow story applies to pines. Spruce, a tougher, longer-grained wood formerly associated with the finest yacht spars, was not the timber wanted for masting a great vessel in our colonial days. The sharp-eyed reader of the story to follow will note that the species *pinus sylvestris,* described as a "fir" by Albion and others, is by its botanical name really a pine. Two types of spruce given the *abies* prefix in my story have the Latin handle of a fir. Why should a tree be of one species to a botanist and another to a 17th century shipbuilder? I don't know. Custom or usage, probably. Possibly ignorance. We have a few misnomers of this kind in our language today. Take Oregon pine, for instance. We know this tree also as "Douglas fir." However, the botanical name for the critter, *pseudotsuga menziesii,* shows it to be some kind of hemlock.

Part I

England

65°N
15°W
10°W
5°W
0°
15°E
20°E
60°N
55°N
50°N
Atlantic Ocean
North Sea
Baltic Sea
the Strait
English Channel
Oslo
Stockholm
Riga
Danzig
Stettin
Hamburg
Amsterdam
London
Plymouth
picea excélsa
pinus sylvestris
S.F.M.

The Wooden Economy

This is a story about ships' masts and mast timber during the period of English settlement in colonial North America. Were it written about our own time, this tale could focus on petroleum with similar overtones of wartime scarcity, international intrigue along the routes of supply, and the willingness of sovereigns to move experts into wilderness regions in order to control the source. The civilized world of today runs on oil. In the 1600's it ran on wood. Wood for virtually everything: architectural structures, transportation conveyances, containers, home fuel, industrial fuel, mine props, basic machinery, tars, dyes etc., each application of wood seeming to breed further need for wood structure or wood products. With early European settlement concentrated on the coasts and waterways, the primeval forests had been mowed back to where timber near the shores was scarce. Overland haulage of timber was expensive or nearly impossible on the mired cart roads of the period. Town populations shivered and froze for lack of affordable fuel in the wintertime. The urban poor were fleeced by woodmongers as were kings who depended upon merchants to supply prime timber for ships.

Most commerce was waterborne in the 1600's. Wooden ships for commerce and for war were built by the thousands among the handful of kingdoms washed by the English Channel. Nations then, like nations today, scrambled and fought to secure the sources of ship timber, mast trees and other so-called naval stores with the vigor that we pursue and protect our sources of oil. Their ships were wind driven. Masts were required to transmit the force of wind via sails into driving power for the hull. Mast timber for large vessels had become scarce and difficult to obtain. For most ship-owning countries, mast timber had become war materiel of the most strategic sort.

England and the Baltic Source

England, at the opening of the 17th century, was a pastoral land with population cut, patched and rewoven by invading armies of north Germans, Danes and French, always from the sea, during the Early Middle Ages. Through five centuries following the Norman invasion of 1066, English kings had solidified control over the heartland of Britain. For three centuries the power of the English monarchy had vied with the provisions of the Magna Carta and the existence of an embryonic Parliament. Coastal trade in small English vessels grew into cross Channel trade. With larger vessels, English merchants adventured into the Baltic, the Mediterranean, around Africa to the back doors of the Levant, and to the rich fishing grounds of Iceland and Newfoundland. Defense of home shores by naval vessels grew into a need for naval protection on the routes of trade. Shipbuilding became profitable. Successful principles of ship design wrested from the Italians, the French and the Dutch became an English science which launched English vessels into the carrying trades long occupied by Continental powers. Shipwrights, caulkers, mast wrights, riggers, ship smiths and coopers led the army of home grown trades, once entirely pastoral, now increasingly mercantile, which moved English goods into overseas markets and sought return cargoes of raw materials.

Thick forests of hardwoods and conifers which covered the greater part of the British Isles in prehistoric times had been pretty well leveled by the 13th century. Certain tracts had been set aside for royal forests to be hunted by the elite or exploited of timber for the royal coffers. But these too were badly

Bedding The Fall

To fell a mast tree took a great deal of skill if collecting the King's bounty was the object of the work. Premature fall would split the trunk if the butt was not adequately severed from the stump. A fall in the wrong direction might hang up, or render the trunk impossible to move. Impact of the fall on bare ground might well shatter the tree.

The felling was therefore carefully planned to allow the tree to drop into a prepared clearing with the butt oriented in the direction the log was to be moved. Deep snow was highly desirable to cushion the impact of the fall. However, since snow cover was required to sled the logs out of the woods, the wise logger had the trees down and ready for removal by the time the snow arrived.

"Bedding" was the term used to denote the preparing of ground for the fall of a big tree. Uneven ground was smoothed with brush. Rocks and stumps were covered by the criss-cross felling of smaller trees. When all was made springy, the axemen began their work at the base of the mast tree.

wasted of shipbuilding timber by the 17th century when England's maritime expansion got into stride. Shortages had begun to develop in shipbuilding materials. Oak, once so plentiful that it had become the only acceptable wood for frame and plank in English fighting ships, had been wantonly destroyed by agriculture and industry without much thought to replenishing the source. Larger ships required larger masts: tremendous poles, a yard thick at the deck and a hundred feet or more in length for a first-rate man-of-war. The rig was extended further upward with a topmast and further yet with a topgallant mast. A ship-rigged vessel of the late 17th century required three lower masts, three topmasts, three topgallant masts, a number of yards to spread sail across the masts, a bowsprit, and a jibboom atop the bowsprit to extend the rig forward of the hull. Masts, yards, bowsprit and jibboom all generally denoted as "spars," required long-grained softwoods for their construction to save weight aloft and to assure suppleness which hardwoods cannot provide. England grew some softwoods, notably firs, suitable for the masts of small vessels and some of the lesser spars in men-of-war and ocean transports. But her soil did not support growth of the huge conifers required for the lower masts and bowsprits of her growing deepwater fleet. These largest spars, collectively termed "masts" in the timber trade, were also sought by England's arch rivals, the Spanish, the French and the Dutch, whose navies and great merchant carriers were also limited by the lack of mast trees on home soil. Navies rose or fell with the ability of home dockyards to fit or replace masts that would stand the crushing force of sail carried in storm or in battle. Expansion of shipbuilding, ocean commerce, and the threat of naval wars at the outset of the 17th century drove England into the Baltic for new supplies of oak, mast timber, and the assortment of fibers, sailcloth and wood oils that constituted naval stores.

Although the states bordering the south and eastern shores of the Baltic Sea had long offered the finest of mast and hull timber to the navies of the world along with the list of lesser wood products of interest to belligerents, they lay bottled behind the narrow strait separating Denmark from Sweden. Access required favorable diplomacy or a strong fleet, and the strait was subject to closure in wartime. Fees, for passage through the strait, were expensive. The trip was a thousand miles one-way to the mast ports. With maritime foes or rivals hovering around to get at the same source of naval supplies, armed convoy was usually necessary to assure delivery. To the cost of the timber in Baltic ports were added the costs of transport, naval protection, bribes, fees, and the profit of the timber contractor who engineered the purchase. Since few English goods were saleable to the Baltic states during those years, costs of the homeward trip were not offset by freights generated on the outbound voyage from England. The convoys sailed essentially empty on the eastward leg.

The Baltic was England's closest source of great masts. To keep the Baltic open for timber trade with England became a focal point of British naval policy in centuries to follow.

Mast Woods

Generations of trial and error had taught English shipbuilders that certain qualities were wanted in timber chosen for masts. These were straightness, suppleness, elasticity, durability, and retention of resin. Of the various softwoods tried, only the North European fir had these qualities. Firs specifically from the middle north European latitudes in a belt extending from the Baltic shore of Poland to the heartland of Russia. Beyond the northern limit of this belt the firs had too little resin to be durable in a spar. Below the southern limit the firs matured too rapidly to build tight grain, and they lost their resin soon after felling. Firs from Norway, Scotland and elsewhere were considered inferior by English shipbuilders and were relegated to last resort or to lesser spars.

For eight hundred years prior to the colonization of North America, the Baltic fir had been floated down the great river systems of eastern Europe and western Russia to the Baltic ports where they were boomed, graded, dressed, and offered to the agents of maritime countries seeking masts and spars. The Baltic fir, sometimes called "Riga fir," had become the British Admiralty's first choice of timber for a great mast. Its resilience and durability were due to the retention of resin long after cutting.

The designation "fir" for the prime mast wood is historic in that trade. The northern European fir is of the genus *pinus sylvestris* — actually a pine. It is known to other trades and in other regions as "scots pine."

Felling

The axes were everything. Saws were not used in the New England woods until the 1890's, more than a century after the last mast pine was felled under the Broad Arrow Policy. Two axemen laid into the tree on opposite sides with the lower, deeper incision dictating the direction of all. The blows fell rapidly. Chips the size of dinner plates flew for a dozen feet as the gleaming axe bits sank nearly to the helve in the soft wood of the white pine. There was pride in the swiftness and the accuracy of the fall, and pride in the planed look of the deepening vee. The heart was reached by the axemen. A shudder went through the great tree. Final blows were dealt. With the cry of "Tim-berrr . . .!" the axemen jumped clear. If skill and judgement were rewarded, the huge pine crashed into the bedded clearing. If it did not, a mast could be shattered or men killed.

The Admiralty's second choice of mast timber was the North American white pine, *pinus strobus*. A shipload of pine masts had been received from Jamestown in 1609 and another from Penobscot Bay in 1634. The North American pine was found to be somewhat inferior in strength to the Baltic fir, but it offered a saving of weight by one fourth. Virgin stands of American pine gave promise of mast sticks of a height and girth long since thinned out from the Baltic source. But although the great masts from across the Atlantic were a boon to shipwrights faced with building masts for the largest ships from smaller sticks of Baltic fir coaked and banded together, the Admiralty was slow to cultivate a North American supply of masts.

The third choice of mast tree was what English seventeenth century shipbuilders called "spruce." Trees of the genus *abies excelsa* of Europe, and *abies nigra* of North America had proven to make good topmasts and yards. Actually firs (from their botanical names), seventeenth century spruce trees large enough for great masts were found to be coarse grained and lacking in youthful toughness. Spruce of any age deteriorated faster than American pine or Baltic fir. Norway spruce was considered best of its kind, good for six years in a spar. However, spars of white pine or Baltic fir were generally good for twice that service.

As great sticks of the Baltic fir became more difficult to obtain, "made" masts were resorted to in the English shipyards. The infinite care required in the fitting, coaking and banding of made masts was a lengthy and expensive process. However, the result was a composite stick well-stressed and made watertight to prevent decay. Arrival of the great pines was a boon to seventeenth century English shipwrights as a single stick could make a lower mast of the largest warship. But as the century progressed and ships-of-the-line grew larger, even the great pines were squared and coaked together in "made" masts. A first-rate warship (100 guns) of the 18th century required lower masts measuring 36 inches diameter at the heel and 120 feet long. Its bowsprit measured 38 inches at the heel, 75 feet long.

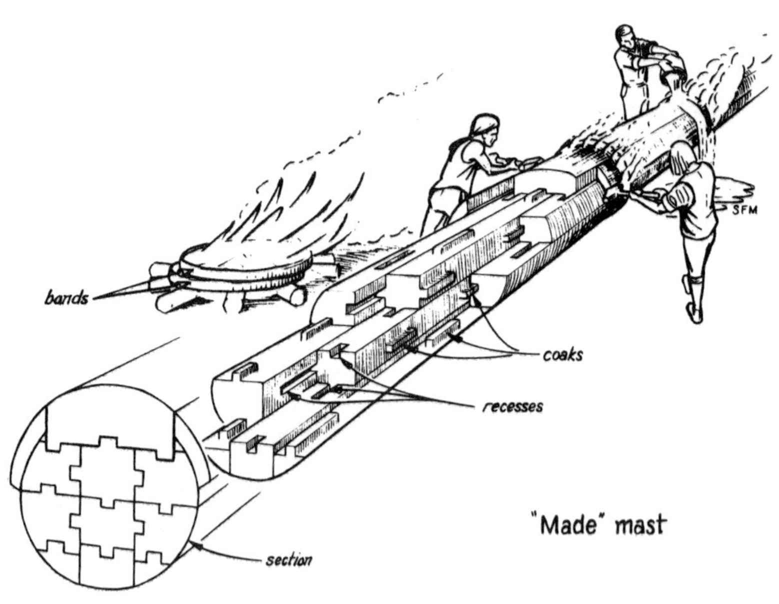

"Made" mast

Growing Need

The British Royal Navy came of age with defeat of the Spanish Armada in 1588. Years of commercial growth and domestic growing pains followed in the opening decades of the 1600's. Empire began with several footholds in India, North America, and several islands in the West Indies. Cross-Channel trade expanded to the Scandinavian countries and into the Mediterranean. Coastal transport of English coal grew into an export industry. British fishing fleets worked the grounds off Iceland and pushed onward to the Grand Banks of Newfoundland and the Gulf of St. Lawrence with more than 300 vessels engaged in the Newfoundland fishery during the third decade. Domestic ship timber, in short supply at the opening of the century, had been supplemented with stepped up imports from the Baltic suppliers. The first two decades had required 100 shiploads of Baltic masts and naval stores annually. By mid-century, when civil war in England had dethroned the king and put the government in the hands of a Puritan Parliament, commercial competition with the Dutch had grown to the breaking point. War followed when the Dutch carriers were shut out of English trade by the Navigation Act of 1651 which forbade importation of goods into England and her colonies except in English ships or ships of the producer country. British trade with the Baltic was threatened by Dutch fleets. With Dutch men-of-war hovering for attack on English ports, and with her own fleet unequipped in-harbor or badly maintained on station for lack of replacement timber, particularly masts, England awoke to the crisis of her timber problem. Great areas of the English economy and the whole of the Royal Navy had grown dependent upon supplies of wood and

Limbing

Axe work again, and quickly done. Most of the limbs of a mast pine were concentrated at the head. A good mast tree had pushed up through a grove of its fellows too tightly spaced to permit much sunlight or air to encourage the growth of branches along the trunk. The head was lopped off at the maximum length to yield a sound spar.

Unlike timber cut for structural purposes where drying of the wood is all important to its stability as lumber, masts were wanted "wet." Suppleness and elasticity were sought in a good spar. A good mast retained these qualities as long as the log retained its resin. Summer and fall cutting insured a tree full of pitch. Retention of the bark was an asset to the future mast as long as the dressing of the spar was done within a reasonable period after delivery to the mast agent. Unbarked at the mast depot, the hewn mast baulks would be stored in the tide.

naval stores regularly obtained from a region over which she had no direct control. Various species of American timber had been brought to England by supply ships returning from the colonies. Accustomed to buying oak in loads directly from the English countryside, and preferring English-grown oak to anything else, the Admiralty had turned down the New England hardwoods as inferior stuff. New England white oak in particular was noted as being too straight for framing timbers and too prone to decay in shipment for shipbuilding purposes at all. Little naval attempt had been made to appraise the hardwoods of the American southern colonies, and the possibilities of live oak, cypress, and long leaf yellow pine as prime shipbuilding timber were missed altogether. But New England pine masts were another matter. The occasional shipload of New England masts arriving in English dockyards before 1650 had bailed the Admiralty out of critical shortage more than once. The pine was light in weight and easy to work. The massive logs, obtainable great sizes only from New England, could be hewn and banded to make a one piece lower mast for a warship of 1650 without resorting to time consuming lamination of smaller pieces. On the eve of the First Dutch War (1652-4) the Admiralty considered a plan to develop a North American source of ship timber and naval stores. The plan was rejected except for masts. To forestall crisis in the replacement of battle-shattered masts and to build a mast timber reserve for warships still on the stocks, mast transports were dispatched by the Admiralty to New England in 1652. Their return in the following season marked the beginning of an annual trade in New England mast timber that was not to cease until outbreak of the American Revolution a century and a quarter later.

The wilderness of North America offered virgin growth timber and the possibility of wood by-products such as tar, pitch, and turpentine to be manufactured by settlers. British development of a North American source of naval stores was seen to be a long term undertaking at best, and probably uneconomic except in the case of masts. Transatlantic distance to the Crown lands of British North America was three times that to the timber ports of the Baltic. Freight costs, for bulk cargo, corresponded. The cost of labor in freehold New England, about six times that of feudal Europe, made American lumber, pitch, tar, turpentine etc. uncompetitive when transatlantic freights were added. There were no developed port facilities in New England for handling timber the size of masts. No means to assure quality such as the time-honored north European "bracking" system. Furthermore, capital investment in settlement, hewing depots or conveyance facilities in the wilderness regions where the mast pines grew ran risk of being wiped out by savages.

Part II

New England

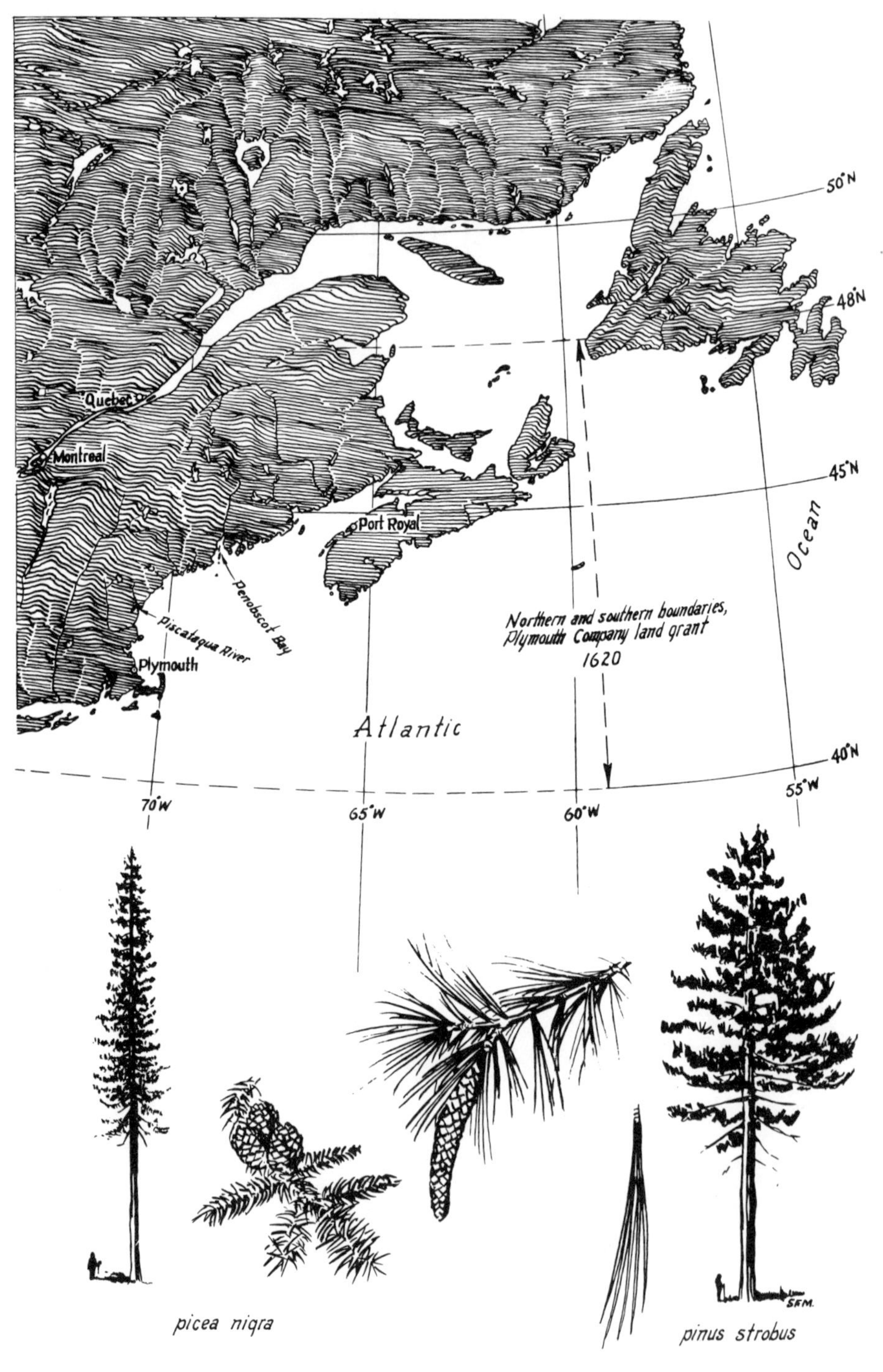

picea nigra

pinus strobus

New England Pines

If the Admiralty was slow in turning to New England for pine masts in the upsurge of overseas trade following defeat of the Armada and close of the Spanish war, it is likely that the prospect was not cheaply to be accomplished. In 1600 there was no commercial trade with North America. To send directly for mast logs was a year's expenditure for ship's charter, ship's crew, timber-cutting crew, and armed guard — with no immunity from Indians, pirates, rival belligerents or the perils of a North Atlantic passage. By 1652 when timber crisis in the shipyards forced the Admiralty to send mast ships directly to New England, there were pockets of settlement and colonials willing to produce any kind of timber for a guaranteed market. Foothold in the wilderness and the beginnings of trade by settlers had taken nearly fifty years to accomplish.

Fully a century of exploration had preceded New England settlement. The early explorers in the wake of Cabot's 1497 voyage upon which Britain had based her North American claim were looking for precious metals or a route to Cathay. Later explorers of the 1500's, usually in the employ of merchants, assayed the coasts and estuaries for commercial exploitation. Breton, Basque and British fishermen mingled with explorers along the coasts of New England and Atlantic Canada. This distant-water fishery, home based in the Old World, was a century old when New England settlement began.

An explorer seeking locations for settlement in 1605 was Capt. George Waymouth, employed by Sir Ferdinando Gorges and others holding proprietory rights in the new country. As Waymouth's vessel, *Archangel,* stood into a river (identified

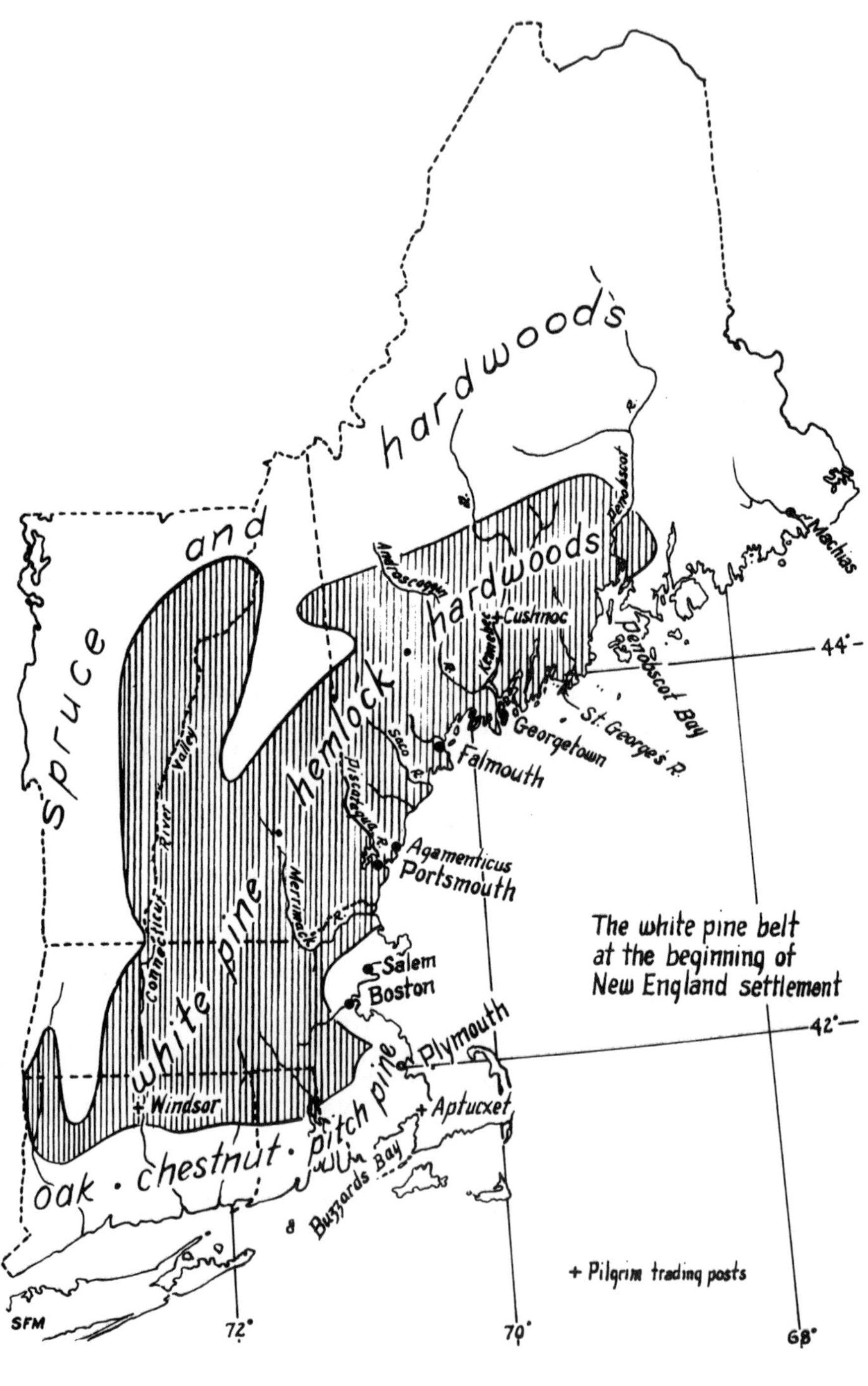

The white pine belt
at the beginning of
New England settlement

today as the St. George, in Maine), James Rosier, chronicler of the voyage, noted of the shore: "The Wood it beareth is no Shrubbish fit only for Fewell, but good tall Firre, Spruce, Birds (birch?), Beech, and Oake . . .". Be as it may, there was plenty of "firre" for ships' masts. Henry Hudson is reported to have cut a fresh foremast for the *Half Moon* on the southern shores of Penobscot Bay in 1609. The first mast shipment of note came from the same region in the *Hercules* of Dover, 1634. Possibly these great sticks were cut from the hills of Camden and Union where Capt. George Waymouth had observed ". . . noteable high timber trees, masts for ships of four hundred tons."

Botanists have shown that the important trees of presettlement New England were deployed approximately in accordance with the accompanying map redrawn from Charles F. Carroll's *The Timber Economy of Puritan New England* (Brown Univ. Press, 1973). Classic view is that the white pines met the sea from Nova Scotia to New Hampshire, and stretched westward, coursing the upper valleys of the Connecticut and the Hudson rivers, and along the St. Lawrence.

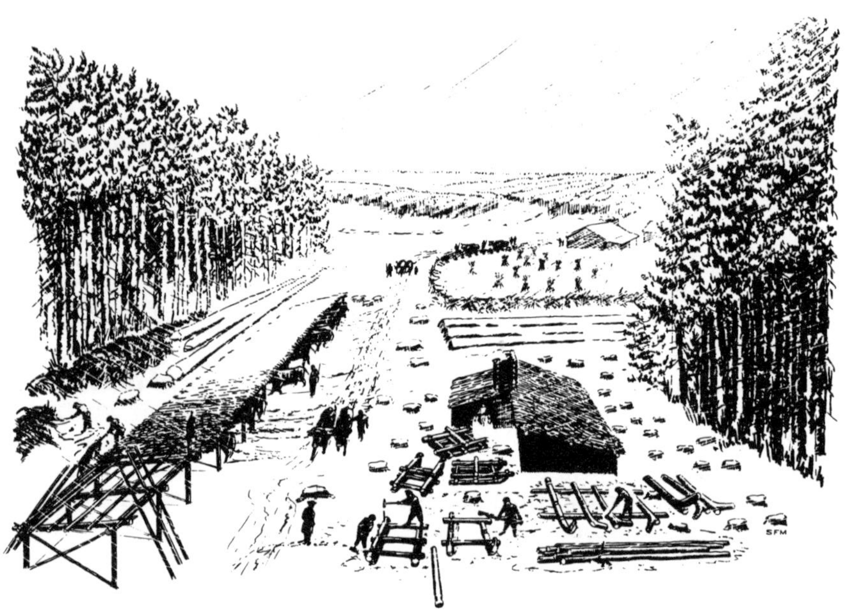

Hovels

The first job upon arrival of crews for winter hauling of timber was the erection of shelters for the draft animals. Animal shelters in the woods were then, as now, called "hovels." They would be quickly erected from any material at hand. Smaller growth pines and the lopped branches from limbed logs would be available in profusion. Bark was often used where barking was done.

This was the time for making sleds or "scoots" upon which the big logs would travel. When time permitted, additional bunk and cooking shelters would be erected for the men in order to relieve the farmhouse of its welcome but burgeoning complement of guests.

Settlement, and the Beginnings of New England Trade

New England of 1620 was a wilderness territory offering little incentive for commercial settlement. The fish were already being taken by home vessels without need of any but temporary shore facilities. Furs, obtained by trade with Indians, were slipping into the hands of the Dutch at New Amsterdam as well as to the French by way of the Acadian settlements and the St. Lawrence. Standing timber was too bulky to cut and assemble for shipment without extensive shore establishment, and timber was too expensive to ship transatlantic without preferential duties in the home market. English colonies to the south of New England had commercial advantage due to their gentler climates and longer growing seasons. Virginia and the Carolinas produced foodstuffs, tobacco, rice and indigo in exportable quantities. Further south, the island colonies of Barbados, Nevis, St. Kitts and (later) Jamaica would give up general cropping for a sure-sell specialty in sugar products. For the London merchant a New England venture meant shiploads of colonist supplies and Indian-trade goods risked against return cargoes of whatever raw products could be mustered by settlers taken to that region. Settlement was tried at the mouth of Maine's Kennebec River in 1607 by the Plymouth Company with colonists led by George Popham. Although some furs were returned by trade with the local Indians, winter hardship and the death of its leader doomed the Popham colony to failure. Foothold on Massachusetts Bay was gained thirteen years later by Pilgrim zealots underwritten (for settlement in Virginia) by an association of English merchants headed by Thomas Weston.

Twitching

The mast road led from the prostrate tree to the nearest waterway. It might be yards or miles in length. At roughly 40 lbs. per cubic foot, a mast log measuring from 3 to 6 feet at the butt and 120 ft. in length might weigh 10 tons. Sleds would support it in three or four places only. The road it traveled had to be prepared very carefully. Stumps and rocks were removed. Soft places were packed with logs and brush. Side hills were cut away and the roadbed wharfed with timber on the downward side. Bridges were built or strengthened. When the snow fell in the late fall, it was packed upon the mast road, wetted down, and frozen solid. Lesser spars made the first trips over the thickening ice road. Then a bowsprit. When the ice road was proved, a mast log was loaded.

To "twitch" a log is to move it over the ground by brute strength without benefit of wheels or runners. It is one of those expressions used by woodsmen which harks back to the mast trade.

Between the Pilgrim arrival in 1620 and the arrival of Admiralty mast ships in 1652 lay three decades of land clearing, hardscrabble farming, and grubbing for return cargoes to pay for supplies sent from England. The 1620's saw returns of furs gained by Pilgrim shrewdness in trading with Indians at truck houses established at the head of navigation on the Kennebec and the Connecticut rivers, and closer to home at the headwaters of Buzzards Bay. Neither the Pilgrims of the 1620's nor the Puritans of the 1630's were versed in seamanship or fishing. A colonial fishing industry got going very slowly due to inexperience and lack of boats. Skilled shipwrights arriving with the flood of Puritan settlers in the 1630's built some shallops for fishing, notably at Salem, but were hampered by lack of capital, nails, cordage, and sailcloth. Lack of money to pay their accustomed wages turned many incoming tradesmen to clearing land for farms. There was some production of hand sawn boards, hand split barrel staves ("clapboards," in older parlance) etc. to send back with the returning immigrant ships, but most incoming trade of the 1630's was the exchange of immigrant possessions for land, cattle, and the materials for new homes. Shipbuilding, to 120 tons, had begun with a few vessels built at Medford, Salem, and on Richmond Island near Casco Bay in Maine. A water-powered sawmill had been established at Berwick, and a tide powered sawmill at Agamenticus. Pine boards, hand split shingles, and clapboards were added to whatever outbound cargoes of dried codfish or farm produce could be accumulated in surplus. English demand for masts and naval stores was well known to the settlers. Although there was some attempt to grow hemp, flax, and to reduce wood to its naval oils, these products never really took hold as a New England product. There is no doubt that some of the mast cargoes returned to England during this period went back with the discharged immigrant ships. However, loading of masts aboard a regular carrier assumes that the tallest trees of the forest have been cut, moved, hewn and assembled for shipment in a hostile, unpopulated region much further east.

The stream of Puritan immigrants which provided New England settlers with trade goods for nearly a decade closed down in the late years of the 1630's. England was in revolution. Religious and civil reforms begun by the Long Parliament gave English Puritans incentive to stay at home. Economic depression was felt in New England as incoming ships continued to land needed goods without offering immigrant demand for homesteading essentials. However, Boston merchants probing the hemisphere for colonist markets had discovered that oak staves and heading for wet storage containers — pipes, hogsheads, casks, barrels — could be sold to wine producers in the Canary and the Azores islands. In fact there was considerable demand for American white oak which made excellent cooperage for the aging and transport of wine. Staves and heading sent to the wine islands returned wine cargoes to the English market where credits could be offset against goods delivered to New England. This first independent New England export was soon extended to the winemakers of Spain and Portugal who welcomed American dried codfish surplus along with the barrel shooks. Colonial fishing effort had increased and was seeking markets. Shipbuilding industry came to life at Boston and Charlestown, and the first vessels constructed were for carrying shaken casks and dried codfish to the wine islands. Docks everywhere were piled high with staves and heading which departed in large shipments along the wine route. Private speculation in masts and trunnels began with a shipment from Boston to England in 1645. Similar shipments were made during the three years following. In 1650 a new and broader market opened for New England merchants striving to get on their feet: staves and heading of porous red oak, for sugar and molasses casks. The island of Barbados had dropped all other crops and stripped the land of timber in favor of sugar production. Oak for cooperage was needed along with structural timber for rolling machinery, mill buildings, slave quarters, wharves, etc. Dried fish was in demand for feeding slaves and mill hands. The opportunity extended to other Caribbean islands which had also converted to sugar production. Returned sugar, molasses and rum cargoes were saleable just about anywhere. By 1652 New England lumbering, shipbuilding, fishing and overseas trading had made a solid start from primitive beginnings just 30 years before. One can only speculate that if the restrictions and incentives of the oncoming Broad Arrow Policy had been applied to New England when the 1630's Puritan immigration slumped, American appetite for competitive enterprise might have died at birth.

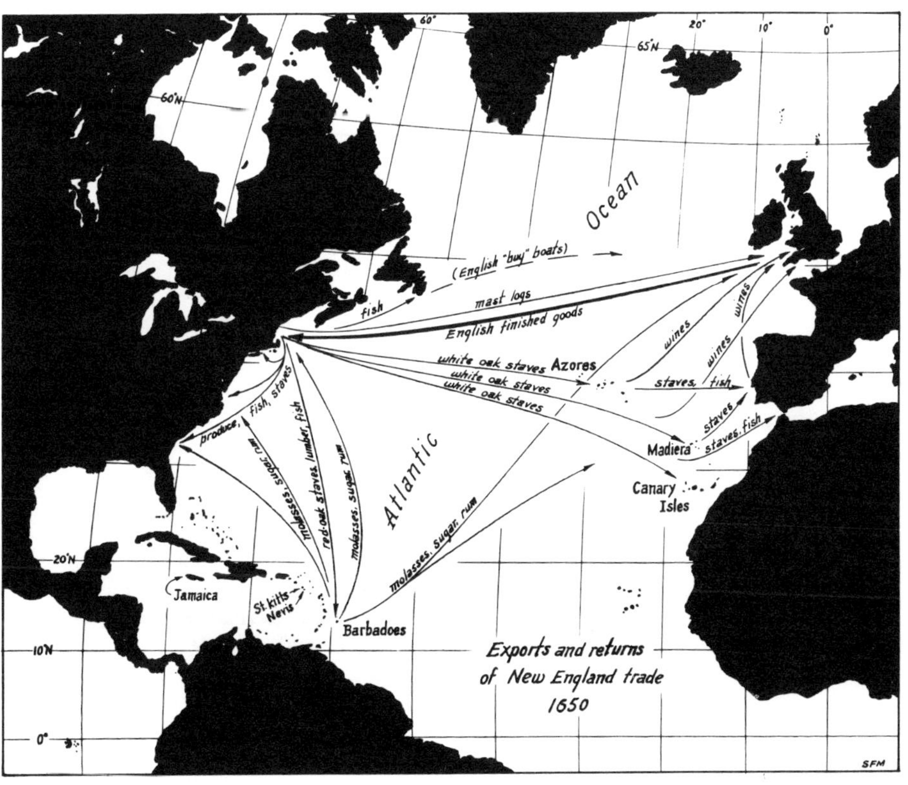

Snub Rope and Bridle Chains

Uphill drawing, or along the flat, was no problem with a ten-ton mast so long as the ice road did not slump under the weight. Downhill required a good deal of skill and forethought. The oxen were usually brought to a halt at the crest of a hill where braking had to be done. Sometimes the downward slope was swept of snow or roughened with straw to increase the friction. Bridle chains, so called, were dragged beneath the runners of the mast scoots. Snub ropes were used, rigged as restraining lines from a sturdy stump or a standing tree. Oxen were deployed behind the load to act as a drogue. This was called "tailing."

Downhill was tough on oxen. If the scoot to which they were yoked was lifted by the long log spanning a depression or rising over the crest of a hill, they hung in the yoke and were strangled. Backs and legs were broken by the chain as the scoot regained earth, dipped into a slump, or lurched off the ice road. Teams were demolished if the snub rope was not smartly handled. The procession was not stopped to replace a killed or injured animal. The dragging beast was cut out of the yoke and another run into its place as the big log moved onward. Spare oxen, with their drovers, were standing by all along the ice road.

The Broad Arrow Policy

With arrival of mast ships dispatched by the Admiralty in 1652, annual shipment of New England masts to English dockyards began. The mast logging effort was well paid. It sought the best trees in the New England pine forest and required undamaged delivery of the whole tree trunk at specified coastal shipping locations. The work took tremendous skill in the felling and in the overland or water delivery of the logs. Hard money was paid for the labor by the London timber contractors. But gold paid for mast logs could not buy food where planting had been neglected, and many a new settlement of farmer/loggers was to experience winter starvation before the lesson was learned.

New England masts were free enterprise in 1652. The Admiralty's move to get mast logs out of the forest produced the labor force, the woods technology, and the holding facilities to make a business of masts along the growing routes of New England trade. Sawmills followed the loggers and took a growing share of the felled pines for conversion to now-merchantable boards, joists and other structural lumber. Since the Admiralty contracts called for supplying Navy dockyards at Antigua and Jamaica as well as England, an extended mast trade with the French colonies in the sugar islands as well as the needs of Spanish shipbuilders along the wine cask route were not ignored by New England merchants. A sound, dressed log for a great mast was frequently worth more than £100 throughout the whole period discussed. If reduced to wide boards, its delivered lumber was saleable for wooden construction at a figure more easily collected by the woodland entrepreneur. With British pressure for dependable delivery of New England pine masts, a wholesale colonial lumber industry began to flourish. By 1685 colonial merchandising of New England white pines had reached a point where the Admiralty felt that strong measures were needed to protect the remaining mast trees in the settled locations as well as further to the east where lumbering was bound to occur. Accordingly a Surveyor of Pines and Timber in Maine was appointed by the Crown to oversee the Admiralty's mast interests in New England. His commission called for a survey of the Maine woods within 10 miles of any navigable waterway as well as the blazing of all suitable mast pines with the King's mark. Appointment of a Surveyor was the first step in the formation of a colonial forest policy.

England had restored the monarchy under two successive Stuart kings. A war with Spain was concluded in 1660, a second war with the Dutch in 1667, and a third war with the Dutch in 1674. There was continuing need for ships' masts as well as a sudden demand for American lumber of any kind following the great London fire of 1666. As William and Mary ascended the throne in 1689, naval construction was stepped up to meet an oncoming struggle with the French. A new timber crisis developed in the dockyards as the growing hostility of Sweden threatened to close passage to the Baltic. To insure a continuing and dependable supply of masts and naval stores from the American colonies, Parliament moved to commandeer the American pines and to control their destruction by mast entrepreneurs, shingle splitters, and sawmill operators. It was basically a mercantilist move to shift timber emphasis from the Baltic where trade was one-sided, and to force the colonials to focus on export of raw materials rather than develop their own competing finished products. Laws de-

Baulking

Baulking is hauling. Hauling of big timber over the roads where wheels or sleds can be used. A baulk is a squared tree trunk. The word goes back to ancient shipwrightery. Mast loggers applied it to the big unhewn pines moving out from the woods.

Masts were sometimes baulked during warm months although moving big timber on a soft road, without snow, was an expensive job. Paired wheels of tremendous diameter were used instead of sleds. The big log was hoisted up and secured under the axles. The galamander of the stonecutters, in later years, was a specialized version of the loggers' wheels.

signed to protect the American pines for exclusive use of the Royal Navy became collectively known as the Broad Arrow Policy. Its symbol, the so-called "broad arrow" (a 3-legged letter A without the horizontal bar), was the ancient mark emblazoned on all property of the Royal Navy including prisoners. The Broad Arrow would be cut into every American pine adjudged suitable for a King's mast by the Surveyor of Pines and Timber. Its shadow hung over all pines in most of the American colonies.

Enacted piecemeal between 1691 and 1729, the Broad Arrow Policy governed New England land rights and woodland activity until outbreak of the American Revolution broke its grip in 1775. Carried to Canada with American loyalists, the Broad Arrow Policy continued to supply masts from the Canadian woods until wooden spars were replaced by iron.

Enabling Acts

The teeth of the Broad Arrow Policy were specific acts of Parliament embodying, on one hand, restrictions on the cutting of trees claimed by the Crown; on the other, incentives in the form of cash bounties (filtered through the London timber contractors) for the cutting and delivery of marked trees. Local extensions of enacted timber restrictions were ramrodded through colonial legislatures by Crown pressure in areas where boundary changes or the terms of original charters gave lumbermen an opportunity to resist.

The initial assertion of Crown proprietorship over standing pines, and Crown authority to interfere with wasteful use of them, is found in the last clause of the new charter granted to Massachusetts by Parliament in 1691. Reserved to the Crown were "all trees of the diameter of twenty four inches and upwards at twelve inches from the ground" growing within Massachusetts territory on ground not previously granted to any private person. The stated penalty was £100 for every such tree cut or destroyed without license from the Crown. These terms served, without much change, as the basis for mast laws in the colonies right up to the Revolution. Blazing of mast trees was begun. To combat resistance of landowners and lumbermen which set in almost immediately, successive acts extended Crown jurisdiction over colonial pines, closed loopholes exploited by the settlers, added cash incentives, and guaranteed a market for American forest products:

A 1699 Order of Council directed the Crown claim on mast pines to all the New England colonies.

The Act of 1704, passed by Parliament as Britain faced shut down of the Baltic source by the Great Northern War, encouraged importation of naval stores from America by means of bounties payable to the importing merchants. £4 per ton for tar and pitch was offered; £3 per ton for "Rozin or Turpentine"; £6 per ton for hemp; and £1 per ton for masts and bowsprits. (A ton was considered to be 40 cubic feet of hewn pine timber, or 50 cubic feet of unhewn). The Navy was to have first choice of all such articles within twenty days of their arrival in Britain. Mast timber and naval stores were thereafter included on the "enumerated" list of colonial export items (which included sugar, tobacco, indigo, cotton and dyewoods) that were to be shipped nowhere but to England.

The Act of 1705 was directed at naval stores. It forbade the cutting of small "Pitch Pine and Tar Trees not being within any Fence or actual Inclosure, under the growth of twelve inches diameter."

The Act of 1711 gave the Surveyor of Pines and Timber authority in all colonies from Maine to New Jersey. Ten years later his power was declared inadequate as colonial merchants found roundabout means to ship mast timber to better buyers in rival countries, and woodsmen found ways to elude the Surveyor and his deputies.

The Act of 1721 extended the restriction to include, ". . . any White Pine Trees not growing within any Township or the Bounds or Limits thereof . . ." This act renewed the bounties (which had lapsed) and removed duties on all forms of American lumber, adding the word "lumber" (an American word, officially recognized for the first time here) to the list of enumerated colonial products tradeable only with England. Terms of the act were extended to Nova Scotia — and to Scotland, to stimulate production of masts and tar in the fir forests there.

The Act of 1729 was a blanket act which modified, recapitulated and re-enacted the provisions of the previous acts which had established the Broad Arrow Policy in the colonies. The bounties on masts and hemp were kept the same whereas those on tar, pitch and turpentine were somewhat lowered. Better enforcement provisions were added to close loopholes that were permitting private property to be created from otherwise Crown lands, or were permitting the escape of acceptable mast logs under some other timber description. The Act of 1729 remained in effect until the outbreak of the American Revolution in 1775.

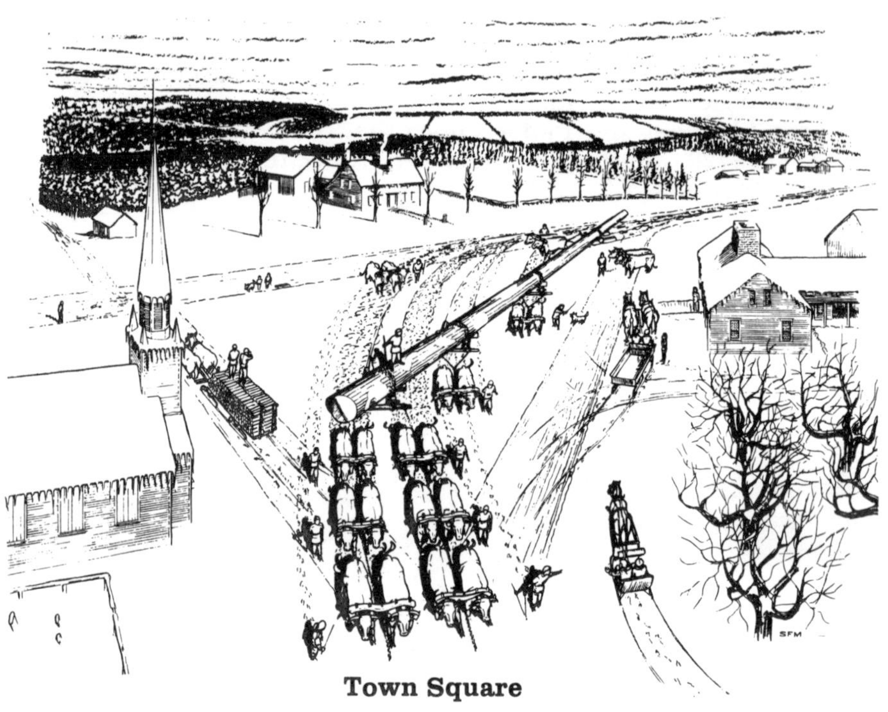

Town Square

Mast roads led straight to the nearest waterway, often through coastal towns. Or, to put it another way, coastal towns in the white pine belt of New England often grew up around roads packed hard by the mast baulkers. Where mast roads met enroute to the landing, the intersection soon described the turning radius of the big sticks. The town "square" of many a New England coastal village owes its peculiar shape to corners clipped by oxen dragging masts in the earliest days.

Gains and Abuses

There was precedent for the Broad Arrow Policy. The French called it *martelage* — the right of naval contractors to mark and cut any tree in the kingdom fit for ship timber. Their policy had been extended to the French settlers in Canada. English kings had exercised similar prerogative within private estates on the English countryside until civil war in 1647 had ended it. Now Parliament had imposed on the English colonies in North America practically the same condition from which its landowning membership had freed itself at home.

Crown claim to certain trees on public lands in North America applied, at first, only to Massachusetts. However, the Massachusetts colony, as defined by the new 1691 charter, combined the old colonies of Plymouth and Massachusetts Bay along with Maine and Nova Scotia. Its territory included the whole shoreline from Cape Cod to Newfoundland with exception of New Hampshire which was governed by a separate charter. Whether certain lands were private or public determined where the Broad Arrow struck.

The various acts specifically excluded trees on private property, yet as dispute continued as to what "private property" implied, royal interpretation gradually rendered the term meaningless. All pines were commandeered in the end. Settlers of the Massachusetts Bay colonies considered the title to their lands to be clear and unreserved. Official answer was that abrogation of the old charter in 1684 had wiped the slate clean, and that the Broad Arrow terms of the 1691 charter now governed. New Hampshire, with its pines threatened by the 1699 Order of Council, was bullied into passing local legis-

Mast Landing

A mast landing was any place reachable by oxen where the mast baulks could be twitched into floating delivery. Tidal marshes were the usual terminus of mast roads during the earliest days. As the cutting moved inland, the big logs were launched into any water draining into the sea which would bear their length and draft. "Mast Landing" still appears as a place name on modern maps of New England.

The mast landing, on tidal water, was the likely place for delivery of the King's timber to representatives of the mast agent. The big sticks were rafted together and towed to the mast depot from here.

lation with terms similar to those in the Broad Arrow clause of the Massachusetts charter. It was in Maine that virtually all land could be called Crown land in the opening decades of the 1700's due to decimation of the settlers by Indian raids.

Maine was in two parts at this time. The province called "Maine" extended only from the Piscataqua River to the Kennebec. Since 1677 it had been governed by Massachusetts under purchase from the heirs of Sir Ferdinando Gorges. The eastern districts, then called "Sagadahoc Territory," were in a flux of ownership between English grantees and the French. It was in Maine that the Surveyor General was to have his most trying moments with the pine-cutting violators. However, the Surveyor's enforcement of the Broad Arrow Policy was considerably helped by the requirement that the fines be split with informers.

A mast pine was not difficult to identify whether it stood on public or private land. It was a tremendous tree which stood head and shoulders above other pines in the forest. If found and scaled by the Surveyor, it was blazed with the King's broad arrow. If not found and marked by the Surveyor, it was still a mast pine and the burden was on you, the cutter, to show where it had come from. The blurred lines of Crown and private ownership inhibited opening land for agriculture if mast pines stood in the way. Until the incentive of cash bounties (Act of 1704) prodded London timber contractors to harvest North American mast pines in any quantity, those pines stood in the way of the landowner, the squatter, and the lumberman until he found a way to remove them without being prosecuted.

Bounties on mast timber at £1 per ton did not begin to approach the market value of those virgin growth trees when exported illegally as spars or cut by night into lumber. Markets for New England lumber continued to grow irrespective of controls by the Crown. Farmers cut the wind screen of lesser trees from around mast pines so that they would be shattered by wind fall in a heavy gale. Marked pines simply dis-

Mast Depot

A mast depot was the established location where the King's pines were assembled, graded, hewn to sixteen sides, and loaded aboard vessels fitted to carry mast baulks within the hull. It was the headquarters of the colonial mast agent who operated under the license of a mast contractor favored by the British Navy Board.

In the left foreground a nearly loaded mast ship is receiving lesser spars on deck while topping off the load below decks with mast baulks pulled upward through the open stern ports. The two vessels at right, floating nearly empty, are loading masts downward from ramps just astern. The long mast house with its crews of hewers is in the middle background of the scene. The view, although conjectural, attempts to show the mast depot which fronted the Fore River on Cleeve's Neck, just below Vaughan's Bridge at Falmouth (now Portland), Maine.

appeared. Their lumber, when found in the sawmills, never measured to the punishable 24-inch width. Fires started mysteriously on Crown lands and rendered scorched pines useless for masts but quite saleable in lumber. Customs officials turned their backs on outgoing cargoes of mast logs listed on the manifests as construction timber. Paper townships sprang up. These were large tracts of wilderness land given to prominent citizens who were to act as absentee proprietors until the townships were populated. As private lands they could be lumbered with impunity. And so it went.

Four decades passed between the new Massachusetts charter of 1691 and the final Broad Arrow act of 1729. Restrictions were laid down, incentives were offered, loopholes were closed. But the law was almost impossible to enforce. No Surveyor with a few deputies could hope to mark all the eligible pines. Their efforts to apprehend woodcutters or to seize logs illegally cut were but token action in a region occupied with land clearing and woods harvest. Virgin growth timber was New England's conspicuous, God-given resource. It rankled second generation Puritan settlers to have agents of the Crown interfere with property rights or to commandeer their best trees. Free market for ships' masts in 1652, spearheaded by the Admiralty's turn to New England, had sent woodchoppers to open timber lands in the eastern river valleys and along the coast of Maine. Forty years of increasing timber export to the world had leveled momentarily when the King laid claim to the whole pine forest. Then it resumed as colonial merchants and lumbermen found ways to get pine timber out of the woods and on to the high seas in some form that passed scrutiny of the Crown's agents. Bounties, payable by the Admiralty under the terms of the 1704 act, helped turn the attention of London timber contractors from the Baltic to New England, but although this was a legal market, it was not the most profitable for the land owners, the ship-owning colonial merchants, or the woodcutters. Back door lumbering of the King's mast trees (after 1691) or the King's pine forests (after 1721) was practiced throughout New England by promi-

Ton Timber

Throughout the ninety year life of the Broad Arrow Policy in colonial New England, the Admiralty paid a normal bounty of £1 per ton of acceptable mast pine. A ton was considered to be forty cubic feet of hewn timber, or fifty cubic feet of timber in the rough.

Crews of hewers laid out the maximum payable dimensions for each pine brought into the mast depot. Each stick was reduced to that size with broadaxe and adze. The contracts specified that the exported masts be "sixteen sided" which is, of course, the shape arrived at when the corners of a squared baulk are removed twice-around. Final shape and taper to the finished mast would be applied by the mastwrights in England.

This scene shows the laying out and hewing of sixteen sides. In practice a big template with comb teeth was probably dragged down the length of the log marking the spaced edges of eight facets as it went. As the log narrowed from butt to head, the "comb" would be dragged diagonally to maintain the narrowing proportion of the eight edges being marked. The work shown here would most likely have been done within the mast house at the rear of the picture.

nent citizens, agents of the Admiralty timber contractors, and some of the less scrupulous Surveyors of Pines and Timber during the whole era of the Broad Arrow Policy. Enumeration of American lumber among the list of items exportable only to England did little to stop the outbound cargoes of New England timber to other parts of the world.

The Broad Arrow Policy succeeded in controlling a supply of mast timber that supplemented the Baltic imports during a crucial century of British naval history. It continued to supply masts from British Canada after the American colonies revolted. If the Admiralty can be commended for forcing expansion of New England woods industry by its quest for masts, the undermining of New England property rights and business morality by the Broad Arrow Policy served mainly to fan sparks of rebellion in the colonists. It is true that Crown attention to American products throughout the duration of the Great Northern War (1700-21) gave New England trade a healthy start, and that the bounties paid under the 1704 act created a profitable naval stores industry in the southern American colonies that might not have materialized otherwise. Yet, trade is trade. Had the offered price been right to begin with, sufficient quantities of New England mast timber would surely have reached England to the exclusion of all other buyers without the need of a restrictive policy.

Mast Ships

The early mast carriers were any vessels looking for homeward cargo. The vessel at the left, in the scene, is one of this early tramp type. She is a Dutch fluyt put into the masting trade near British colors. Her rig and headwork date her to about 1650, or about 100 years earlier than the setting of this scene. However, the fluyt was reputed to be a fast sailer and a good carrier. Vessels of this class appear quite late in contemporary American port scenes.

The middle vessel is a snow of about 1750. The vessel loading from the water at right is a mast ship of proportions likely to have evolved in this particular trade during the hundred year span of the Broad Arrow Policy.

The place pictured is meant to be the mast depot on Cleeve's Neck, Falmouth, Maine, around 1750. The mast ships are carefully fleshed out from the hull lines of contemporary vessels in Chapman's *Architectura Navalis Mercatoria,* a Swedish manual of ship design published in 1768.

Mast Agents and Surveyors

English masts had always come from abroad. Mast timber had been purchased throughout the years from London contractors who retained agents in the Baltic ports where suitable sticks were assembled for export. When North America was turned to for a fresh supply of bigger wood, it was these same mast contractors who obtained license to cut American pines reserved for the King.

Mast agents for the London contractors took up residence in New England. Some of their names became linked with the future of the region: Samuel Waldo, mast agent at Boston; Mark Hunking Wentworth, mast agent at Portsmouth; Thomas Westbrook, to be succeeded by George Tate, mast agent at Falmouth (now Portland); and Edward Parry, at Georgetown (now Bath). Nothing prevented these mast agents from setting up as lumber merchants on their own accounts. Most of them became rich and powerful men in their respective colonies. The mast agents were, in a sense, New England managers of commercial enterprises based in London. They were not King's officers, but licensees of licensees permitted to harvest the Crown timber.

The King's man in New England was the Surveyor of Pines and Timber in Maine. He was given four deputies. Appointments to this post began in 1685. At first the surveys extended ten miles inland from any navigatable waterway. Then as the trees disappeared and the need for them continued, the Surveyor and his deputies sought to range the whole of the pine belt from Nova Scotia westward to the St. Lawrence. In the beginning their duty was to survey the stands, mark the suit-

Stern Port

Here's a close up of the fluyt's stern during the initial loading of mast cargo. The open port next to the rudder (there's one on each side of the sternpost) is grossly oversize compared to ports normally cut to receive timber into the hold of a vessel. With the loading just begun, the vessel is still quite light with the timber port some feet from the water's edge. When the load is completed, the port would be closed and caulked.

Notice the problems entailed in the shipboard loading of mast baulks. With no cargo aboard, a vessel lay high in the water with her stern ports elevated. The ingoing spar would have to run upward to the stern port and then downward into the hull. Tons of weight were involved. As the vessel filled with baulks and settled downward with her ports nearer the water, the masts would be run straight in. As she topped her load beneath decks the open stern ports were nearly awash. She would have to receive the masts upward into the hull, probably from the water.

able trees, report their locations, and to instruct the colonists in the growing of hemp and the making of tar. These duties were to be carried on in addition to their main employment as customs agents. The tree work soon got out of hand. Production of tar and hemp never became interesting to the New England colonists.

The King's Surveyor was hardly popular with the New England colonists. The office was badly paid to begin with, and the area to be covered by this officer and his four deputies was tremendous. It was work enough just to find and mark the trees which tended to disappear when the incisors of the Broad Arrow had passed through. Swamp law governed the future of informers. The colonial courts increasingly sided with the violators as conditions slid toward the Revolution.

One Surveyor deserves mention in the era before that office fell into the hands of the Wentworth family at Portsmouth. This was John Bridger. Bridger was a former shipwright who sincerely believed that the King's Navy could be well served with the forest products of North America. He did his job too well in the wake of lesser appointees who had been lax, disinterested, absentee, or involved in the timber harvest themselves. Bridger conducted extensive and accurate surveys and he locked horns with the backwoods mast pine hijackers for twenty-five years. His reward was to be dropped from the King's payroll in favor of someone with better connections at home.

The Admiralty's avenues for purchasing ship timber had always been rank with politics, graft, and the costs of private monopoly gained by the contractors. The King's masts, from North America, were no exception. When the fumes cleared, Portsmouth, New Hampshire was the center of the mast trade; Governor Benning Wentworth of New Hampshire was the Surveyor General; and his brother, Mark Hunking Wentworth, was mast agent at Portsmouth, N.H., with powerful ties to the Navy Board at home. During Benning Wentworth's administration from 1743 to 1766, the Broad Arrow Policy was

The Hold

During the era of the Broad Arrow Policy, the mast transports ranged from 400 to 600 tons burthen. At least one mast ship is reported to have measured 1000 tons. Cargoes of 30 to 50 mast baulks were recorded along with lesser spars dunnaged between or carried on deck.

This scene exhibits the reconstructed interior of the "single deck flyboat for transporting timber for masts," hull lines of which are given in Plate 27 of *Architectura Navalis Mercatoria*, Sweden, 1768. What's different about this fly-boat (variously: "flight," "flute," "fluyt") design for a mast transport is that she is completely open inside. The other vessels of this size shown in Chapman are well braced athwartships with one or more decks spanning the hull below the main deck. From the standpoint of stowage, lower decks would be no asset in a mast carrier.

If the scale for the fly-boat is read correctly, she appears to be a vessel 115 ft. long, 27 ft. maximum breadth, and with 13 ft. depth of hold. The hull is fitted with a capstan extending downward to the keelson. Large stern ports are the only other feature which distinguish this mast ship from other carriers portrayed. The open fore hatch was probably covered with a grating when the capstan was manned on deck. The men shown in the scene are scaled at about 5 ft. in height.

softpedaled while townships were sold under the authority of the Governor, and the marked timber within them was merchandised selectively by his brother. The Wentworth brothers extended their control into the pine forests of the upper Connecticut, the upper Hudson, and well into the old Gorges patent in Maine. It was John Wentworth, Benning's nephew, who succeeded into the Governorship and the Surveyor General's office in 1766, and who put the administration of the Broad Arrow Policy back onto the footing of tireless, vigorous, and consistent enforcement which harked back to the efforts of John Bridger.

But the lands drained by the Piscataqua had been stripped of mast pines to the White Mountains by then. During the summer of 1761 and again in 1762, forest fire destroyed a wide swath of the finest mast pines that Portsmouth and Falmouth had been drawing upon. The burnt area extended from the woods of New Hampshire to the shores of Casco Bay, a distance of some fifty miles. The mast loggers moved east to new settlements as far down the coast as Machias. By 1772 the main volume of mast exports had passed into George Tate's jurisdiction at Falmouth, Maine.

Outbreak of the Revolution ended the Broad Arrow Policy in New England. In April, 1775, news of Bunker Hill and Lexington stopped all shipments of masts to the King. Waiting mast cargoes were seized by the colonists at Portsmouth, Falmouth and Georgetown. The load of mast baulks seized by the colonists from the mast ship *Minerva* was reported to be rotting in Portland harbor fifty years later.

Mast logging as a marine trade did not end in New England with eclipse of the Broad Arrow Policy. Pine masts continued to be cut and shipped by Yankee traders to whomever would buy them at the highest price. France was a good customer for New England masts during the Revolution. England continued to import them, although on a commercial basis, after the war had ended. But the King had other trees in North America. Until about 1825, great pines marked with the broad arrow continued to move out of the valleys of the Saint John and the Mirimichi to the King's depot at Halifax. Administrator of the Broad Arrow Policy in Canada was former New Hampshire Governor, John Wentworth, Loyalist.

Departure

Mast timber was highly prized material of war. The Dutch, the French and the Spaniards were delighted to seize an English mast ship during the whole era of the Broad Arrow Policy. Mast ships usually sailed in convoy with an armed vessel.

The mast ships were the ocean liners of their day. Westbound they carried manufactured goods and immigrants to the colonies. Eastbound they packed in passengers returning to England. Passengers must have camped atop the dunnaged masts because the one known plan of a mast ship shows an open hold with no accommodations whatsoever.

This scene looks westward along the Fore River at Falmouth, Maine. The King's mast depot is in the background at right. Three loaded mast transports are preparing to get underway in convoy.

Select Bibliography

Adams, S.	*The History of Bowdoinham, Maine* (Fairfield, Me. 1912)
Albion, R. G.	*Forests and Sea Power* (Cambridge, Mass. 1926)
Baker, W. A.	*A Maritime History of Bath, Maine.* Vol. I (Bath, Me. 1973)
Bamford, P. W.	*Forests and French Sea Power* (Toronto, 1956)
Bradbury, C.	*The History of Kennebunkport, Maine* (Kennebunk, Me. 1837)
Baugh, D. A.	*Naval Administration, 1715-1750* (Navy Records Society, London, 1977)
Carroll, C. F.	*The Timber Economy of Puritan New England* (Providence, R. I. 1973)
Chapman, G. W.	"Mast Industry of Old Falmouth", in *Maine Historical Society Collections,* 2nd series, vii, 390-405
Davis, R.	*The Rise of the English Shipping Industry* (Devon, 1962)
Drisko, G. W.	*The History of Machias, Maine* (Machias, 1904)
Goold, W.	*Portland in the Past* (Portland, 1886)
Gould, A. T.	*The St. Georges River* (Portland, 1950)
Hatch, L. C.	*Maine, A History* (New York, 1919)
(Simon & Schuster)	*The International Book of Wood* (New York, 1976)
Kellogg, E.	*Good Old Times* (Boston, 1898)
Malone, J. J.	*Pine Trees and Politics* (London, 1964)
McLellan, H. D.	*The History of Gorham, Maine* (Portland, 1903)
Malone, J. J.	"England and the Baltic Naval Stores Trade in the Seventeenth and Eighteenth Centuries" *The Mariner's Mirror,* LVIII, 1972, pp. 375-395.
Otis, J.	*The Story of Old Falmouth* (New York, 1901)
Pike, R. E.	*Tall Trees, Tough Men* (New York, 1967)
Ridlon, G. T.	*Saco Valley Settlements* (Portland, 1895)
Rowe, W. H.	*The Maritime History of Maine* (New York, 1948)
Thurston, F. G.	*Three Centuries of Freeport, Maine* (Freeport, 1940)
Willis, W.	*Journals of the Rev. Thomas Smith and the Rev. Samuel Deane* (etc.) (Portland, 1849)